PRETHISTORIC ANIMALS

KNOW ABOUT EXTINCT ANIMALS

NAFAY BAKSH

ISBN 979-888546336-2

Contents

CHAPTER ONE

Woolly Mammoth

Woolly mammoths lived during the last ice age, and they may have died off when the weather became warmer and their food supply changed. Humans may also be partly responsible for their disappearance due to hunting. Although the word "mammoth" has come to mean "huge," woolly mammoths were probably about the size of African elephants. Their ears were smaller than those of today's elephants. This was probably an adaptation to the cold climate that kept their ears closer to their heads and kept them warmer. Their tusks were very long, about 15 feet (5 meters) and were used for fighting and digging in the deep snow. Mammoths were herbivores and ate mostly grass, but also ate other types of plants and flowers.The woolly mammoth (Mammuthus primigenius) is a species of mammoth that lived during the Pleistocene until its extinction in the Holocene epoch. It was one of the last in a line of mammoth species, beginning with Mammuthus subplanifrons in the early Pliocene. The woolly mammoth began to diverge from the steppe mammoth about 800,000 years ago in East Asia. Its closest extant relative is the Asian elephant. DNA studies show that the Columbian mammoth was a hybrid between woolly mammoths and another lineage descended from steppe mammoths. The appearance and behaviour of this species are among the best studied of any prehistoric animal because of the discovery of frozen carcasses in Siberia and Alaska, as well as skeletons, teeth, stomach contents, dung, and depiction from life in prehistoric cave paintings. Mammoth remains had long been known in Asia before they became known to Europeans in the 17th century. The origin of these remains was long a matter of debate, and often explained as being remains of legendary creatures. The mammoth was identified as an extinct species of elephant.Climate change, not humans, was reason woolly mammoths went extinct, research suggests. ... From there, they determined melting icebergs killed off the woolly mammoths. When the icebergs melted, vegetation – the primary food source for the animals – became too wet, thus wiping the giant creatures off the face of the planet .

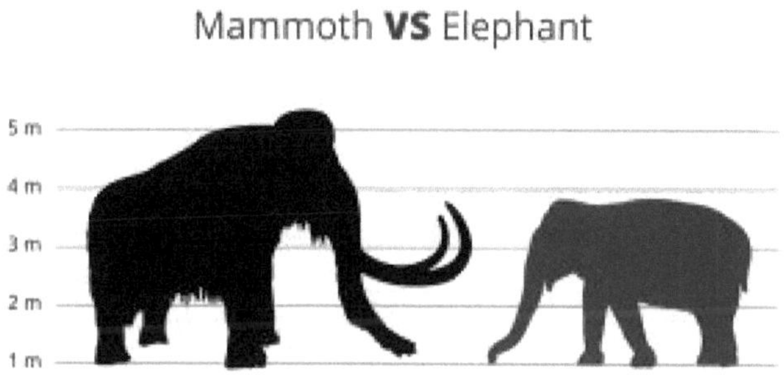
Mammoth VS Elephant
5 m
4 m
3 m
2 m
1 m

CHAPTER TWO

Smilodon

Smilodon is a genus of the extinct machairodont subfamily of the felids. It is one of the most famous prehistoric mammals and the best known saber-toothed cat. Although commonly known as the saber-toothed tiger, it was not closely related to the tiger or other modern cats. Smilodon lived in the Americas during the Pleistocene epoch (2.5 mya 10,000 years ago). The genus was named in 1842 based on fossils from Brazil; the generic name means "scalpel" or "two-edged knife" combined with "tooth". In North America, Smilodon hunted large herbivores such as bison and camels, and it remained successful even when encountering new prey species in South America. Smilodon is thought to have killed its prey by holding it still with its forelimbs and biting it, but it is unclear in what manner the bite itself was delivered. Scientists debate whether Smilodon had a social or a solitary lifestyle; analysis of modern predator behavior as well as of Smilodon’s fossil remains could be construed to lend support to either view. Smilodon probably lived in closed habitats such as forests and bush, which would have provided cover for ambushing prey. Smilodon died out at the same time that most North and South American megafauna disappeared, about 10,000 years ago. Its reliance on large animals has been proposed as the cause of its extinction, along with climate change and competition with other species, but the exact cause is unknown.

Smilodon was a large animal that weighed 160 to 280 kg (350-620 lbs), larger than lions and about the size of

Siberian tigers. Smilodon was different from living large cats, with proportionally longer front legs and a much more muscular build. Its upper canine teeth are long, flat and daggerlike.

CHAPTER THREE

Giant ground sloth

Human activity may have caused giant sloths and other large mammals in North America to go extinct 11,000 years ago. Around 11,000 years ago, saber tooth cats, woolly mammoths, giant ground sloths, and almost every other large mammal in North America went extinct.Megatherium is an extinct genus of ground sloths endemic to South America that lived from the Early Pliocene through the end of the Pleistocene.Megatherium americanum is one of the largest land mammals known to have existed, weighing up to 4 t (4.4 short tons) and measuring up to 6 m (20 ft)

in length from head to tail. It is the largest-known ground sloth, as big as modern elephants, and would have only been exceeded in its time by a few species of mammoth. Megatherium species were members of the abundant Pleistocene megafauna, large mammals that lived during the Pleistocene epoch.Megatherium had a narrow, cone-shaped mouth and prehensile lips that were probably used to select particular plants and fruits. Megatherium also possessed the narrowest muzzle of all ground sloths from the Pleistocene, possibly meaning it was a very selective eater, able to carefully pick and choose which leaves and twigs to consume.The first fossil specimen of Megatherium was discovered in 1788 by Manuel Torres, on the bank of the Luján River in Argentina. The fossil was shipped to Museo Nacional de Ciencias Naturales in Madrid the following year, where it remains. It was reassembled by museum employee Juan Bautista Bru, who also drew the skeleton and some individual bones.Megatherium inhabited woodland and grassland environments of the lightly wooded areas of South America, with a Late Pleistocene range centred around the Pampas where it was an endemic species, as recently as 10,000 years ago. Megatherium was adapted to temperate, arid or semiarid open habitats.

Megalonyx sloths grew to around 9.8 feet (3 meters) long and weighed up to 2,205 lbs.

CHAPTER FOUR

Woolly Rhinoceros

Genetic analysis of the remnants of 14 woolly rhinos shows that a warming climate, not hunting, probably killed them off 14,000 years ago. The numbers of woolly rhinos remained constant until close to their extinction, and far after humans had migrated to their territory in Siberia.The remarkably preserved carcass of an Ice Age-era woolly rhino has been unearthed by locals in eastern Siberia, researchers have said. ... The rhino is believed to have lived in the late Pleistocene era, anywhere between 20,000 and

50,000 years ago.The woolly rhinoceros (Coelodonta antiquitatis) is an extinct species of rhinoceros that was common throughout Europe and Asia during the Pleistocene epoch and survived until the end of the last glacial period. The woolly rhinoceros was a member of the Pleistocene megafauna.The woolly rhinoceros was covered with long, thick hair that allowed it to survive in the extremely cold, harsh mammoth steppe. It had a massive hump reaching from its shoulder and fed mainly on herbaceous plants that grew in the steppe.Mummified carcasses preserved in permafrost and many bone remains of woolly rhinoceroses have been found. Images of woolly rhinoceroses are found among cave paintings in Europe and Asia.Woolly rhinoceroses mostly fed on grasses and sedges that grew in the mammoth steppe. Its long, slanted head with a downward-facing posture, and tooth structure all helped it graze on vegetation. It had a wide upper lip like that of the white rhinoceros, which allowed it to easily pluck vegetation directly from the ground. Pollen analysis shows it also ate woody plants (including conifers, willows and alders), along with flowers, forbs and mosses.Isotope studies on horns show that the woolly rhinoceros had a seasonal diet; different areas of horn growth suggest that it mainly grazed in summer, while it browsed for shrubs and branches in the winter.The woolly rhinoceros lived mainly in lowlands, plateaus and river valleys, with dry to arid climates, and migrated to higher elevations in favourable climate phases. It avoided mountain ranges, due to heavy snow and steep terrain that the animal could not easily cross. The rhino's main habitat was the mammoth steppe, a large, open landscape covered with wide ranges of grass and bushes. The woolly rhinoceros lived alongside other large herbivores, such as the woolly mammoth, giant deer, reindeer, saiga antelope and bison – an assortment of animals known as the Mammuthus-Coelodonta Faunal Complex.With its wide distribution, the woolly rhinoceros lived in some areas alongside the other rhinoceroses Stephanorhinus and Elasmotherium.

An adult woolly rhinoceros typically measured 3 to 3.8 metres (9.8 to 12.5 ft) from head to tail, with an estimated weight of around 1,800–2,700 kg (4,000–6,000 lb) or 2,000 kg (4,400 lb). It grew up to 2 m (6.6 ft) tall at the shoulder, about the same size as the white rhinoceros.

CHAPTER FIVE

Arsinoitherium

Arsinoitherium is an extinct genus of paenungulate mammals belonging to the extinct order Embrithopoda. It is related to elephants, sirenians, hyraxes and the extinct desmostylians. Arsinoitheres were superficially rhinoceros-like herbivores that lived during the late Eocene and the early Oligocene of northern Africa from 36 to 30 million years ago, in areas of tropical rainforest and at the margin of mangrove swamps. A species described in 2004,

A. giganteum, lived in Ethiopia about 27 million years ago.Arsinoitherium, genus of extinct large, primitive, hoofed mammals that have been found as fossils in Egypt in deposits from the Eocene Epoch (56 million to 34 million years ago) and elsewhere in deposits from the Oligocene Epoch (34 million to 23 million years ago).Arsinoitherium was a hefty creature with thick, hairless skin resembling elephant hide. Arsinoitherium was very selective in the types of fruit and leaves it ate.

At approximately 6 feet tall and 11 feet long, Arsinoitherium zitteli is similar in size and shape to the White Rhinoceros. With its giant twin horns, it looks like a fanciful version of a rhino, however, it is not closely related to rhinos at all.

CHAPTER SIX

Short faced bear

The short-faced bear (Arctodus sp.) is an extinct bear genus that inhabited North America during the Pleistocene epoch from about 1.8 Mya until 11,000 years ago. It was the mostcommon tremarctine bear in North America and many of its fossils have been found in the La Brea tar pits in southern California.[1] There are two recognized species: the lesser short-faced bear (Arctodus pristinus) and the giant short-faced bear (Arctodus simus), with the latter considered to be one of the largest known terrestrial mammalian carnivores that has ever existed. It has been hypothesized that their extinction coincides with the Younger Dryas period of global cooling commencing around 10,900 BC.The short-faced bears belong to a group of bears known as the Tremarctinae, which appeared in North America during the earliest parts of the late Miocene epoch in the form of Plionarctos, a genus considered ancestral to Arctodus. During the Great American Interchange that followed the joining of North and South America, tremarctines invaded South America, leading to the evolution of Arctotherium and the modern spectacled bear (Tremarctos ornatus). Although the early history of Arctodus is poorly known, it evidently became widespread in North America by the Kansan age about 800,000 years ago.The short-faced bear became extinct about 11 000 years ago. The cause is perhaps partly the earlier extinction of some of the large herbivores that it may have preyed upon or scavenged, and partly increased competition with the smaller grizzly bear that entered North America from Eurasia.The short-faced bear or bulldog bear (Arctodus) is an extinct genus of bear endemic to North America during the Pleistocene era about 1.8 million years ago (mya) to 11,000 years ago. At that time, Arctodus simus may have been one of the largest mammals that lived on land and ate meat.

Enter Caption

CHAPTER SEVEN

Dire wolf

The dire wolf is an extinct canine. It is one of the most famous prehistoric carnivores in North America, along with its extinct competitor Smilodon. The dire wolf lived in the Americas and eastern Asia during the Late Pleistocene and Early Holocene epochs (125,000–9,500 years ago). The species was named in 1858, four years after the first specimen had been found.Dire wolves were one of the most common and most widespread carnivores in North America during the Pleistocene, ranging from coast to coast, from Florida and Mexico to southern Canada. Many of Ohio's other large Ice Age mammals were uncovered years ago in the state.By comparing the ancient DNA to genetic material from other canids, they found the dire wolf's closest living relative was the African jackal, which diverged about 5.1 million years ago, while the closest living wolves diverged about 5.7 million years ago.Most scientists agree that the dire wolf specialised in hunting large herbivores, many of which – including horses, bison and camels – became extinct or drastically declined in North America around 13,000 years ago. The disappearance of their prey almost certainly drove the dire wolf extinct.The dire wolf was about the same size as the largest modern gray wolves.The dire wolf was a formidable predator, measuring almost five feet from head to tail and weighing in the vicinity of 150 to 200 pounds—about 25 percent bigger than the biggest dog alive today (the American mastiff), and 25 percent heavier than the largest gray wolves.With an estimated maximum weight of 200 pounds, dire wolves would have balanced the scale with the average adult male in the United States. The smaller A. guildayi subspecies, however, would share a weight range with the average 13-year-old.Dire wolves, with reddish fur, facing off against gray wolves. ... Weighing around 150 pounds, the creatures were larger than the heaviest of today's gray wolves. They roamed throughout large swaths of the Americas and preyed on now extinct megafauna, such as Ice Age horses and ground sloths.

CHAPTER EIGHT

Mastodon

Enter Caption

A mastodon is any proboscidean belonging to the extinct genus Mammut that inhabited North and Central America during the late Miocene or late Pliocene up to their extinction at the end of the Pleistocene 10,000 to 11,000 years ago. Mastodons lived in herds and were predominantly forest-dwelling animals.Mastodons disappeared from North America as part of a mass extinction of most of the Pleistocene megafauna, widely believed to have been caused by a combination of climate changes at the end of the Pleistocene combined with overexploitation by Clovis hunters.Despite the superficial resemblance, mastodons were distinct from mammoths. Mastodon were shorter and stockier than mammoths with shorter, straighter tusks. ... Mammoths were grazers, their molars have flat surfaces for eating grass.While similar in size and stature, fossil evidence shows that mastodons were slightly smaller than mammoths, with shorter legs and lower, flatter heads. ... Both animals were herbivores, but mastodons had cone-shaped cusps on their molars designed to crush leaves, twigs and branches.While mastodons look a lot like modern elephants, they are not closely related. The ancestors of modern elephants and mammoths went their separate ways about 5 million years ago, and mastodons branched off even earlier, about 25 million years ago.Mastodons, which first appeared on earth around 20 million years ago, pre-date mammoths, which arrived some four to five million years ago. Mastodons also became extinct first, departing about 12,700 years ago.high at the shoulder, mastodons had long tusks they used to break branches and uproot plants. They were hunted for food by Paleo-Indians. ... The simplest answer is they became extinct, meaning that eventually all the mastodons died off. Scientists think there are two possible reasons: climate change and overhunting.

9 798885 463362

Printed by Libri Plureos GmbH in Hamburg,
Germany